1000

First Words
in French

Learning French

Learning a new language is fun. The best way to learn French is to go to a country where it is spoken all around you. Talking with someone who knows the language very well is good, too. If possible, share this book with a grown-up who will help you to pronounce the words properly and ask you the questions under each picture.

You may notice some ways in which French is different from English. In English, there is only one word for **the**. We say **the house** and **the castle**. In French, there are two different words – **la maison** and **le château**. If you are talking about more than one thing, the word for **the** is **les**. Each time you learn a new word in French, try to learn the word for **the** that goes with it.

In the same way, **a house** and **a castle** are **une maison** and **un château**. **Some houses** and **some houses** are **des maisons** and **des châteaux**.

You may also notice that some French words have little signs above or below the letters. These help you to pronounce the word in the right way.

Have fun learning French!

1000

First Words in French

Text by Nicola Baxter and Guillaume Dopffer

Illustrated by Susie Lacome

ARMADILLO

This paperback edition printed in 2008

© 2001 Bookmart Limited

ISBN: 978-1-84322-385-6

5 7 9 10 8 6 4

Published by Armadillo Books, an imprint of
Bookmart Limited, Registered Number 2372865
Trading as Bookmart Limited, Blaby Road,
Wigston, Leicester, LE18 4SE, England

Produced for Bookmart Ltd by
Nicola Baxter
PO Box 215, Framingham Earl,
Norwich, NR14 7UR

Editorial Consultant: Ronne Randall
Designer: Amanda Hawkes

Printed in Singapore

Sommaire

La Maison

 une poubelle

 un seau

 une boite à outils

 une jardinière

 un toît

 une gouttière

 un chemin

 une cheminée

 une échelle

 une fenêtre

 une porte

Who is in the garage?
Is the bucket blue?
Can you see two gloves?
Where are Teddy Bear's boots?

une radio

un pas de porte

une bouteille thermos

une collation

des briques

une tuile

une treille

un projecteur

une allée

une sonnette

une serviette

une antenne

un gant

Qui est dans le garage?
Le seau est-il bleu?
Peux-tu trouver deux gants?
Où sont les bottes d'Ursule L'Ourson?

La Cuisine

un bol-doseur

une casserole

un livre de cuisine

un grille-pain

un rouleau à pâtisserie

un bocal

un réfrigérateur

une cuillère en bois

une poêle

un torchon

un four à micro-ondes

What is on the worktop?
Can you see the lid for the saucepan?
Who is looking in the fridge?
What could you use for mixing?

un plan
de travail

un tabouret

une
cuisinière

une bouilloire

un fer
à repasser

un évier

un robot
ménager

du liquide
vaisselle

un tiroir

un pense-bête

un lave-vaisselle

un égouttoir

Qu'y a-t-il sur le plan de travail?
Peux-tu trouver le couvercle de la casserole?
Qui fouille dans le réfrigérateur?
De quoi pourrais-tu te servir pour mélanger?

un bol-mixeur

La Chambre à Coucher

un lit

une penderie

une commode

une table
de chevet

un pyjama

une robe de
chambre

un oreiller

une brosse
à cheveux

une
couette

un mobile   un peigne

What can you see in Teddy Bear's bedroom?
What is under the bedside table?
What colour are Teddy's pyjamas?
What is on the table?

des pantoufles

des chaussettes

un coffre

un poster

un cerf-volant

un illustré

un abat-jour

une toise

une corbeille

un réveil

un dessin

un cintre

une tirelire

Que vois-tu dans la chambre d'Ursule L'Ourson?

Qu'y a-t-il sous la table de chevet?

De quelle couleur est le pyjama d'Ursule l'Ourson?

Qu'y a-t-il sur la table?

La Salle de Bains

 un savon

 une serviette

 une éponge

 une brosse à dents

 une baignoire

 un lavabo

 du papier toilette

 une douche

 un rideau de douche

 un tapis de bain

une armoire à pharmacie

What colour are the wall tiles?
What is on the bath mat?
How many toothbrushes can you count?
How many pawprints can you see?

des toilettes

 un miroir

 une brosse à ongles

 un robinet

 une balance

 une serviette de bain

 du shampooing

 du bain-moussant

 un tube de dentifrice

 un jouet de bain

 des carreaux

 une brosse

 un canard

De quelle couleur sont les carreaux au mur?
Qu'y a-t-il sur le tapis de bain?
Combien de brosses à dents comptes-tu?
Combien de traces de pattes vois-tu?

Le Salon

un tapis

un fauteuil

une bibliothèque

un magazine

un aspirateur

une plante verte

un chiffon
à poussière

une
pendule

un rideau

un
lampadaire

un coussi

What is on the sofa?
How many dusters can you see?
What is on the bookcase?
What colour is the armchair?

un journal un vase un magnétoscope une photo de la moquette un tableau une table basse

une télécommande

un canapé

une cheminée

une télévision

une chaîne hi-fi

du papier peint

Qu'y a-t-il sur le canapé?
Combien de chiffons y a-t-il?
Qu'y a-t-il sur la bibliothèque?
De quelle couleur est le fauteuil?

Le Grenier

un berceau

une maison de poupée

une cage

une lucarne

une boite en carton

un cadre

une valise

un mannequin

des skis

une ampoule

une toile d'araignée

How many jamjars can you see?
What is on the sledge?
Can you see a bed?
What is red and white?

16

de la
peinture

un transat

des
bouteilles

un chapeau

des pots
à confiture

une trappe

une canne à
pêche

un fauteuil
à bascule

des décorations
de Noël

une machine
à coudre

un cheval
à bascule

des patins
à glace

une luge

Combien de pots à confiture vois-tu?
Qu'y a-t-il sur la luge?
Vois-tu un lit?
Qu'est-ce qui est rouge et blanc?

Le Jardin

 une fourche

 du gazon

 une tondeuse à gazon

 des graines

 une brouette

 des cisailles

 de la terre

 une pelle

 un pot

 un arrosoir

 un tuyau d'arrosage

What is on the grass?
What is in the wheelbarrow?
How many birds can you see?
What colour is the watering can?

18

des feuilles

 un nichoir

 une binette

 une fourche

 une truelle

 un perchoir

 une cabane

 une jardinière suspendue

 un râteau

 une haie

 des fleurs

 une fontaine

 un balai

Qu'y a-t-il sur l'herbe?
Qu'y a-t-il sur la brouette?
Combien d'oiseaux vois-tu ?
De quelle couleur est l'arrosoir?

La Rue

une bicyclette   un pigeon   des bonbons   un gâteau

un trottoir

une grille

un lampadaire

une poubelle

un camion de livraison

un chauffeur

une poussette

How many wheels can you see?
Which shop sells lollies?
What colour are the boots in the shoe shop?
Do you like cakes?

une école

une pâtisserie

un paquet

une route

une sucette

une bouche d'égout

un casque

un sac à provisions

un magasin de chaussures

un panneau

une confiserie

une corde à sauter

des bottes

Combien de roues vois-tu?
Quel est le magasin qui vend des sucettes?
De quelle couleur sont les bottes dans le magasin
   de chaussures?
Aimes-tu les gâteaux?

21

Le Supermarché

un porte-monnaie

de l'argent

des fruits

un sac à main

des boites de conserve

un client

un caddie

une queue

un panier

un sac

une caisse-enregistreuse

How many bears are in the queue?
Can you see Teddy Bear?
Where is the milk?
What is on the conveyor belt?

du lait

 des clés

 un yaourt

 un carton

 du jus de fruits

 du miel

 un code barre

 un vendeur

 un ticket de caisse

 un panneau

 un caissier

 des légumes

 un tapis de caisse

Combien d'ours y a-t-il dans la queue?
Peux-tu voir Ursule L'Ourson?
Où est le lait?
Qu'y a-t-il sur le tapis de la caisse?

L'École

une règle

un tableau noir

une carte
géographique

des crayons

de la pâte
à modeler

de la craie

des patères

une
maîtresse

des feutres

du papier

de l'eau

What is the teacher holding?
What do you need for painting?
How many pupils can you see?
What colour is the ruler?

un élève

un pinceau

une gomme

un portrait

un aquarium

un chevalet

une boîte de couleurs

l'alphabet

a b c d e
f g h i j k l
m n o p q
r s t u v w
x y z

a b c d e
f g h i j k l
m n o p q
r s t u v w
x y z

un cahier

un ordinateur

un cartable

un puzzle

Que tient la maîtresse?
De quoi as-tu besoin pour peindre?
Combien d'élèves vois-tu?
De quelle couleur est la règle?

des ciseaux

25

La Ferme

un mouton   un agneau   un
cochon

un
cochonnet

des poussins

une poule

un chien

un cheval

un poulain

un fermier

une ferme

Where is the duck?
What is the farmer holding?
How many chicks does he have?
Is the tractor yellow?

un canard

 un caneton

 un chat

 une souris

une barrière

une clotûre

 un épouvantail

 une mare

 un coq

 une vache

 un veau

 un champ

 un tracteur

Où est le canard?
Que tient le fermier?
Combien de poussins a-t-il?
Est-ce que le tracteur est jaune?

Le Parc

un cornet
de glace

un toboggan

une balançoire

un coureur

un bac à sable

une fontaine

un parterre
de fleurs

un banc

des
genouillères

un oiseau

un klaxon

Is Teddy Bear on the swing?
What is in the hamper?
How many bears are wearing helmets?
How many wheels does a tricycle have?

un tricycle

 une planche à roulettes

 une bascule

 des roues

 une malle

 un cerceau

 une balle

 un pique-nique

 un écureuil

 des sandwiches

 une trottinette

 des patins à roulettes

 un baladeur

Ursule L'Ourson est-il sur la balançoire?
Qu'y a-t-il dans la malle?
Combien d'ours portent des casques?
Combien y a-t-il de roues sur un tricycle?

Le Monde des Contes

une baguette magique

un puits magique

un champignon

un elfe

une fée

une lance

un bouclier

une couronne

une épée

un dragon

une armure

un chevalier

une princesse

Who can do magic?
What colour is the dragon?
Where does a king live?
Who wears armour?

une bannière

un chapeau-claque

un page　　　une citrouille

un magicien

une cape

un prince　　une reine　　un roi

un géant　　un château

Qui peut faire de la magie?
De quelle couleur est le dragon?
Où vit un roi?
Qui porte une armure?

La Campagne

une tente

un arbre

un randonneur

un pont

une forêt

une montagne

un champ

une rivière

un lac

une branche

un feu de camp

How many carriages does the engine have?
Who is sitting on a log?
Is the sleeping bag in the tent?
Is the rowing boat on the river?

un tronc

une
locomotive

un wagon

un buisson

des jumelles

une
cascade

une souche

un village

un rail de
chemin de fer

une barque

une colline

un sac de
couchage

des rochers

Combien de wagons sont derrière la locomotive?
Qui est assis sur une souche?
Le sac de couchage est-il dans la tente?
La barque est-elle sur la rivière?

Le Port

des
poissons

des
pagaies

une corde

une balise

des hublots

un sous-marin

un paquebot

un pêcheur

une grue

un chalutier

un bateau
à moteur

What can go under the water?
What are round windows on a boat called?
How many fish can you see?
What is on the jetty?

un gilet de sauvetage

un crochet

une ancre

un homard

un mat

un kayak

du ski nautique

un casier à homard

une combinaison

une jetée

un porte-conteneurs

un plongeur

une bouée de sauvetage

Qu'est-ce qui va sous l'eau?
Comment appelle-t-on les fenêtres rondes sur un bateau?
Combien de poissons vois-tu?
Qu'y a-t-il sur la jetée?

37

L'Aéroport

une cane

une boisson

un chariot à bagages

un tableau d'affichage

un bus

un avion

une tour de contrôle

des toilettes

un hangar

une étiquette

un porte-papiers

How many suitcases can you see?
Who is carrying a mop?
Can you see our Teddy Bear?
Have you ever been in an aeroplane?

une valise   un café   une piste d'atterrissage   un balai à franges   un agent d'entretien   des billets   un appareil photo

une manche à air

un pilote

un comptoir d'enregistrement

une hôtesse

un sac à dos

un téléphone

Combien de valises vois-tu?
Qui porte un balai à franges?
Vois-tu Ursule L'Ourson?
As-tu déjà pris l'avion?

L'Hôpital

 un plateau

 une infirmière

 de l'eau

une bande

 un drap

un médecin

 une robe de chambre

un médicament

 un visiteur

 un déambulateur

 de la ouate

What is the nurse holding?
Who is in the lift?
Is the doctor's coat red?
Have you ever been in hospital?

un
ascenseur

un
infirmier

une
montre

une écharpe

un
pansement

une
seringue

une couverture

une carte

un plâtre

une courbe de
température

un
stéthoscope

un
thermomètre

Prompt
Rétabliss
ement!

Que tient l'infirmière?
Qui est dans l'ascenseur?
La blouse du médecin est-elle rouge?
As-tu déjà été dans un hôpital?

un fauteuil
roulant

Le Magasin de Jouets

une dinette

une boîte à surprises

des crayons de couleur

une toupie

une maison

un jeu de société

une marionnette

un boulier

des quilles

un chateau-fort

une poupée

How many building blocks can you see?
Who is holding a glove puppet?
Which toys are for babies?
Which is your favourite toy?

44

des perles

un chariot

un yoyo

des dés

des billes

un robot

des cônes

des briques

une chenille

des soldats

un livre de
coloriage

une voiture
à pédales

un costume
de clown

Combien de briques vois-tu?
Qui tient une marionette?
Quels jouets sont pour les bébés?
Quel est ton jouet préféré?

L'Atelier

une clé   une   une tasse   une
lampe-torche   perceuse

une poche

un calendrier

une étagère

une poignée
de porte

un mètre-
mesureur

des biscuits

l'arche de Noé

46

How many animals can you see?
What is on the workbench?
What is on the shelf?
What colour is the door?

une scie

 un tournevis

 des vis

 des clous

 un marteau

 des lunettes

 un canif

 du papier de verre

 un maillet

 une planche

 des animaux

 une pince

 un établi

Combien d'animaux vois-tu?
Qu'y a-t-il sur le plan de travail?
Qu'y a-t-il sur l'étagère?
De quelle couleur est la porte?

Le Bord de Mer

un drapeau

du sable

un coquillage

la mer

un château de sable

une étoile de mer

un maillot de bain

un parasol

des galets

une épuisette

des lunettes

How many legs does a starfish have?
How many sea shells can you see?
What is very cold?
What colour is the flag?

un crabe

 des palmes

 un voilier

 des brassards

 le soleil

 des vagues

 de la lotion solaire

un phare

 une bouée

 un ballon de plage

un caleçon de bain

  une mouette

une glace à l'eau

Combien de branches une étoile de mer a-t-elle?
Combien de coquillages vois-tu?
Qu'est-ce qui est très froid?
De quelle couleur est le drapeau?

Les Saisons

le printemps

l'été

l'automne

l'hiver

Which season is it now?
Is there snow in the summer?
When does Teddy Bear fly his kite?
What comes from clouds?

La Météo

 le soleil

 la neige

 l'arc-en-ciel

 la glace une bourrasque

 des stalactites

 le vent

 un flocon

 un nuage

 une tornade

 un bonhomme de neige

 la pluie

 la rosée

 la foudre

la chaleur

 l'innondation

 le givre

 le brouillard

le froid

 des flaques

Quelle est la saison en ce moment?
Y a-t-il de la neige en été?
Quand Ursule L'Ourson fait-il voler son cerf-volant?
Qu'est ce qui vient des nuages?

Mes Aliments Préférés

 du beurre

 un biscuit

des céréales

 du sucre

 de la soupe

 un hotdog

des frites

 des sauces

du chocolat

du riz

des beignets

des spaghettis

What is your favourite food?
Do you like cheese?
How many spoons can you see?
What is on Teddy Bear's ears?

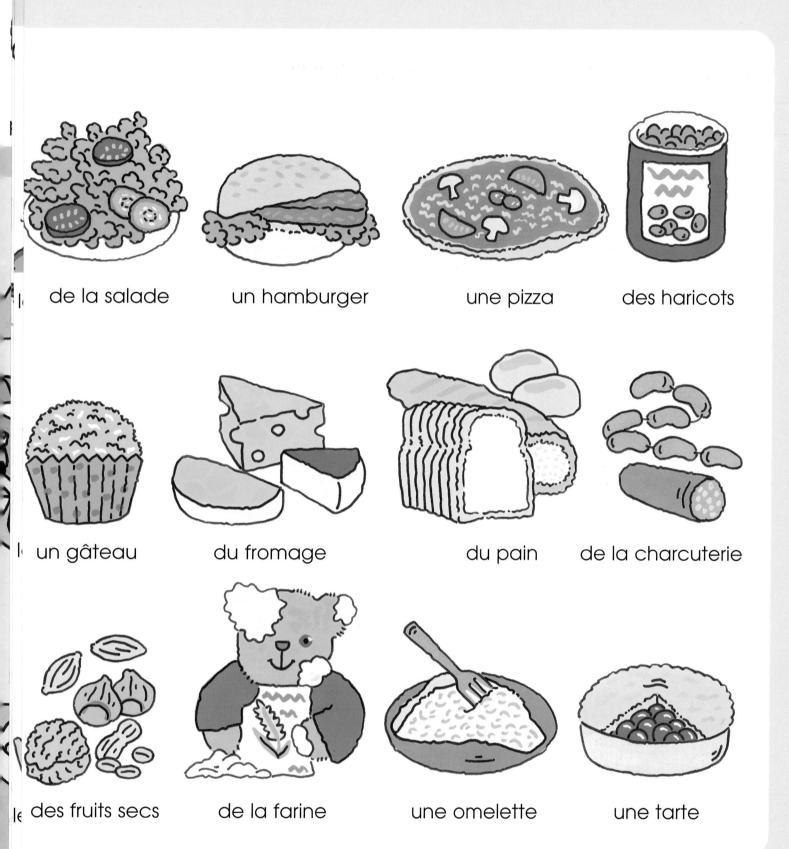

de la salade

un hamburger

une pizza

des haricots

un gâteau

du fromage

du pain

de la charcuterie

des fruits secs

de la farine

une omelette

une tarte

Quel est ton plat préféré?
Aimes-tu le fromage?
Combien de cuillères vois-tu?
Qu'y a-t-il sur les oreilles d'Ursule?

Les Nombres

une maison

deux voitures

trois cerf-volants

quatre lapins

cinq ballons

six canards

sept fraises

huit crayons

neuf fleurs

dix coeurs

What colour are the rabbits?
How many bears can you see?
How many flowers can you count?
What is five plus seven?

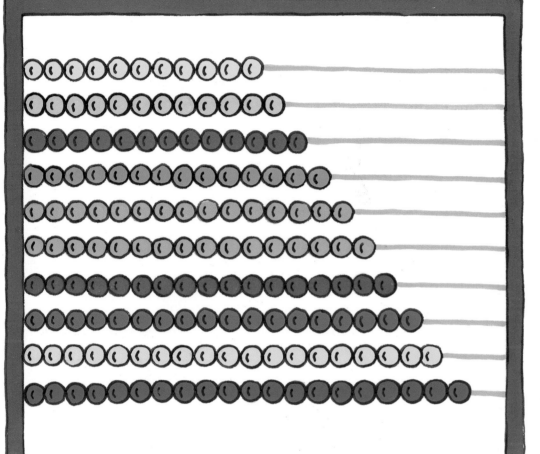

11 onze
12 douze
13 treize
14 quatorze
15 quinze
16 seize
17 dix-sept
18 dix-huit
19 dix-neuf
20 vingt

100 cent

troisième   second   premier

De quelle couleur sont les lapins?
Combien d'ours vois-tu?
Combien de fleurs comptes-tu?
Combien font cinq plus sept?

Les Couleurs

blanc

noir

jaune

marron

violet

orange

bleu marine

bleu

rouge

gris

rose

vert

What is your favourite colour?
What colour is Teddy Bear's top?
Are there zigzags on Teddy Bear's trousers?
Which shape is pink?

Les Formes

 un cœur

 des rayures

 un cercle

 un carré

une étoile

un losange

 un rectangle

 des zigzags

 des pois

 un ovale

un triangle

 un damier

Quelle est ta couleur préférée?
De quelle couleur est le tricot d'Ursule?
Il y a-t-il des zigzags sur le pantalon d'Ursule?
Quelle forme est rose?

69

Les Fruits

une framboise

des grains
de raisin

des myrtilles

une figue

une mangue

de la rhubarbe

une groseille

une poire

une
banane

de la
pastèque

une lime

Which is your favourite fruit?
How many bananas can you see?
What is Teddy Bear holding?
Which fruits are red?

74

une
orange

une pêche

un
citron

une prune

un
abricot

une cerise

une
pomme

une papaye

un
pamplemousse

une fraise

des airelles

une clémentine

un ananas

Quel est ton fruit préféré?
Combien de bananes vois-tu?
Que tient Ursule L'Ourson?
Quels fruits sont rouges?

Les Légumes

des champignons

une carotte

des broccolis

un poivron rouge

des petits pois

un poireau

un épi de maïs

un oignon

une pomme
de terre

un chou-fleur

des tomates

du céleri

Do you like carrots?
What is Teddy Bear eating?
Which vegetables are green?
What is your favourite vegetable?

une laitue

une betterave

des flageolets

un panais

un concombre

des radis

une patate douce

des haricots verts

un navet

des herbes

un chou

une courgette

Aimes-tu les carrottes?
Que mange Ursule L'Ourson?
Quels légumes sont verts?
Quel est ton légume préféré?

Les Fleurs

un coquelicot

un iris

une marguerite

une campanule

une pensée

une jonquille

un dahlia

un tournesol

un œillet

un lys

une rose

Which flowers are yellow?
Which flower grows very tall?
What is under the cup?
What is Teddy Bear holding?

À Table!

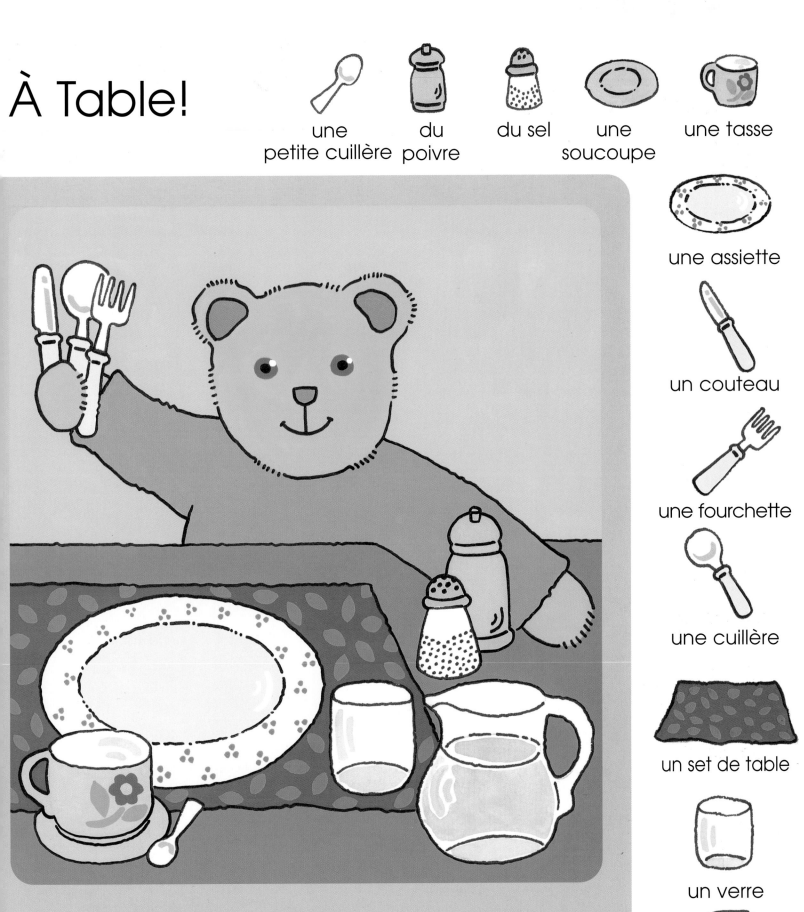

une petite cuillère

du poivre

du sel

une soucoupe

une tasse

une assiette

un couteau

une fourchette

une cuillère

un set de table

un verre

une carafe d'eau

Quelles fleurs sont jaunes?
Quel est la fleur qui pousse le plus haute?
Qu'y a-t-il sous la tasse?
Que tient Ursule L'Ourson?

Les Contraires

lent

rapide

grand

petit

grand

petit

ouvert

fermé

allumé

éteint

au pied

au sommet

Is an elephant small?
Is this book open or shut?
Are you inside or outside?
Are balloons heavy?

en haut   en bas   usé   neuf

plein   vide   léger   lourd

dedans   dehors   mince   gros

Les éléphants sont-ils petits?
Ce livre est-il ouvert ou fermé?
Es-tu à l'intérieur où à l'extérieur?
Les ballons sont-ils lourds?

Les Oiseaux

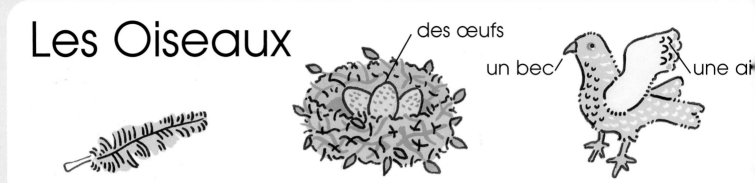

des œufs

un bec

une a[i]

une plume

un nid

un hibou

un macareux

un toucan

un pingouin

un paon

une autruche

un émeu

What is in the nest?
How many beaks can you see?
Which birds are black and white?
Which birds are eating fishes?

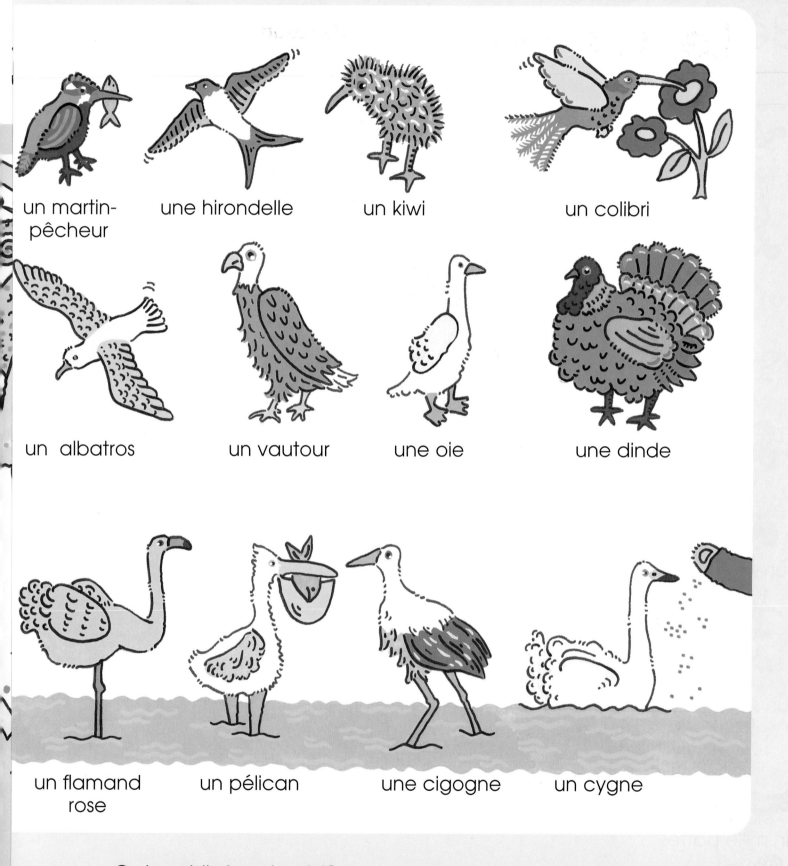

un martin-pêcheur

une hirondelle

un kiwi

un colibri

un albatros

un vautour

une oie

une dinde

un flamand rose

un pélican

une cigogne

un cygne

Qu'y a-t-il dans le nid?
Combien de becs vois-tu?
Quels oiseaux sont noir et blanc?
Quels oiseaux sont en train de manger des poissons?

Les Animaux Sauvages

un koala

un rhinocéros

un tatou

un kangourou

un ours blanc

un gorille

une girafe

un singe

un tigre

un éléphant

un serpent

un panda

Which animal is very talll?
Which animal is very big?
Which animal is Teddy Bear feeding?
Which is your favourite animal?

un raton-laveur   un bison   un porc-épic   un zèbre

un ours   un crocodile   un chameau   un lion

un loup   un léopard   un castor   un hippopotame

Quel animal est très grand?
Quel animal est très gros?
Quel animal Ursule L'Ourson est-il en train de nourrir?
Quel est ton animal préféré?

Les Animaux Domestiques

une niche un chaton un hamster un clapier

un canari

un lapin

un perroquet

une perruche

un cochon d'Inde

de la nourriture pour poisson

un poisson rouge

Do you have a pet?
Who lives in a kennel?
Where is the rabbit?
What is in the fish tank?

un chiot

 des bulles

une brosse

 une tortue

un os

 une laisse

un collier

 une écuelle pour chien

un panier à chat

 un aquarium

 une trappe

 une tortue marine

 de l'eau

As-tu un animal domestique?
Qui vit dans une niche?
Où est le lapin?
Qu'y a-t-il dans l'aquarium?

89

Les Mots

a

abacus   *un boulier*
aerial   *une antenne*
aeroplane   *un avion*
alarm clock   *un réveil*
albatross   *un albatros*
alphabet   *l'alphabet*
anchor   *une ancre*
angry (to be)   *être fâché*
animals   *des animaux*
ankle   *la cheville*
anorak   *un anorak*
ant   *une fourmi*
apple   *une pomme*
apricot   *un abricot*
aquarium   *un aquarium*
archery   *le tir à l'arc*
arm   *le bras*
armadillo   *un tatou*
armbands   *des brassards*
armchair   *un fauteuil*
armour   *une armure*
ashamed (to be)   *avoir honte*
aunt   *une tante*
autumn   *l'automne*

b

baby alarm   *une alarme*
baby record book   *un livre de bébé*
back   *le dos*
baggage trolley   *un chariot à bagages*
ball   *une balle*
balloon   *un ballon*
banana   *une banane*
bandage   *une bande*
banjo   *un banjo*
banner   *une bannière*
barcode   *un code barre*
baseball   *le baseball*

basketball   *le basketball*
bath   *une baignoire*
bath mat   *un tapis de bain*
bathroom cabinet   *une armoire à pharmacie*
bathroom scales   *une balance*
bath towel   *une serviette de bain*
bath toy   *un jouet de bain*
beachball   *un ballon de plage*
beads   *des perles*
beak   *un bec*
beans   *des haricots*
bear   *un ours*
beaver   *un castor*
bed   *un lit*
bedside table   *une table de chevet*
bee   *une abeille*
beetle   *un scarabée*
beetroot   *une betterave*
bench   *un banc*
bib   *un bavoir*
bicycle   *une bicyclette*
big   *grand*
binoculars   *des jumelles*
bird   *un oiseau*
bird table   *un perchoir*
birthday cake   *un gâteau d'anniversaire*
birthday card   *une carte d'anniversaire*
biscuit   *un biscuit*
black   *noir*
blanket   *une couverture*
blindman's buff   *colin-maillard*
blouse   *un chemisier*
blue   *bleu*
bluebell   *une campanule*

blueberries   *des myrtilles*
board book   *un livre cartonné*
board game   *un jeu de société*
bone   *un os*
bookcase   *une bibliothèque*
bootees   *des botons*
boots   *des bottes*
bored (to be)   *s'ennuyer*
bottles   *des bouteilles*
bottom (body)   *les fesses*
bottom (position)   *au pied*
bow   *un nœud*
bow tie   *un nœud-papillon*
branch   *une branche*
bread   *du pain*
bricks   *des briques*
bridge   *un pont*
broad beans   *des flageolets*
broccoli   *des broccolis*
broom   *un balai*
brother   *un frère*
brown   *marron*
brush   *une brosse*
bubble bath   *du bain-moussant*
bubbles   *des bulles*
bucket   *un seau*
budgerigar   *une perruche*
buffalo   *un bison*
buggy   *une poussette*
building blocks   *des briques*
bulldozer   *un bulldozer*
buoy   *une balise*
bus   *un autobus*
bush   *un buisson*
butter   *du beurre*
butterfly   *un papillon*
button   *un bouton*

c

cabbage   *un chou*
cage   *une cage*
cake   *un gâteau*
cake shop   *une pâtisserie*
calendar   *un calendrier*
calf   *un veau*
camel   *un chameau*
camera   *un appareil photo*
camp fire   *un feu de camp*
camper van   *un camping-car*
canary   *un canari*
candle   *une bougie*
canoe   *un kayak*
cans   *des boîtes de conserve*
car   *une voiture*
card   *une carte*
car transporter   *un camion à plateau*
caravan   *une caravane*
cardboard box   *une boîte en carton*
carnation   *un œillet*
carpet   *de la moquette*
carriage   *un wagon*
carrier bag   *un sac*
carrot   *une carotte*
carton   *un carton*
cashier   *un caissier*
castle   *un château*
cat   *un chat*
cat basket   *un panier à chat*
cat flap   *une trappe*
caterpillar   *une chenille*
cauliflower   *un chou-fleur*
celery   *du céleri*
cello   *un violoncelle*
centipede   *un scolopendre*
cereal   *des céréales*

chain *une chaîne*

chalk *de la craie*

chalkboard *un tableau noir*

chameleon *un caméléon*

changing bag *un sac à langer*

changing mat *un matelas à langer*

check-in desk *un comptoir d'enregistrement*

checks *un damier*

cheek *la joue*

cheese *du fromage*

cherry *une cerise*

chest (box) *un coffre*

chest of drawers *une commode*

chicks *des poussins*

chimney *une cheminée*

chips *des frites*

chocolate *du chocolat*

Christmas decorations *des décorations de Noël*

chrysalis *une chrysalide*

circle *un cercle*

cleaner *un agent d'entretien*

climbing *l'escalade*

clipboard *un porte-papiers*

cloak *une cape*

clock *une pendule*

cloth book *un livre en tissu*

clothes peg *une pince à linge*

cloud *un nuage*

clown *un clown*

clown outfit *un costume de clown*

coach *un autobus*

coat *un manteau*

coat hooks *des patères*

coathanger *un cintre*

cockerel *un coq*

coffee *un café*

coffee table *une table basse*

cold *le froid*

collar *un collier*

coloured pencils *des crayons de couleur*

colouring book *un livre de coloriage*

comb *un peigne*

comic *un illustré*

computer *un ordinateur*

conductor *un chef d'orchestre*

container ship *un porte-conteneurs*

control tower *une tour de contrôle*

conveyor belt *un tapis de caisse*

cookbook *un livre de cuisine*

cookies *des biscuits*

coral *du corail*

cot *un berceau*

cotton wool *de la ouate*

courgette *une courgette*

cousin *une cousine (un cousin)*

cow *une vache*

crab *un crabe*

cradle *un berceau*

cranberries *des airelles*

crane *une grue*

crawling *ramper*

crayons *des crayons*

cricket *le cricket*

crocodile *un crocodile*

crown *une couronne*

cucumber *un concombre*

cuddling *faire des câlins*

cuddly toy *une peluche*

cup *une tasse*

curtain *un rideau*

cushion *un coussin*

cycling *le vélo*

cymbals *des cymbales*

d

daffodil *une jonquille*

dahlia *un dahlia*

daisy *une marguerite*

dancing *danser*

deck chair *un transat*

delivery van *un camion de livraison*

dew *la rosée*

diamond *un losange*

dice *des dés*

digger *une pelleteuse*

dishwasher *un lave-vaisselle*

diver *un plongeur*

diving *le plongeon*

doctor *un médecin*

dog *un chien*

dog bowl *une écuelle pour chien*

doll *une poupée*

doll's house *une maison de poupée*

dolphin *un dauphin*

door *une porte*

doorbell *une sonnette*

doorknob *une poignée de porte*

doorstep *un pas de porte*

doughnuts *des beignets*

down *en bas*

dragon *un dragon*

dragonfly *une libellule*

drain *une bouche d'égout*

draining board *un égouttoir*

drawer *un tiroir*

drawing *un dessin*

dressing *s'habiller*

dressing gown *une robe de chambre*

dressmaker's dummy *un mannequin*

drill *une perceuse*

drink *une boisson*

drinking *boire*

drinking straw *une paille*

driver *un chauffeur*

driveway *une allée*

drying *se sécher*

duck *un canard*

duckling *un caneton*

dumper truck *un camion-benne*

dungarees *une salopette*

dustbin *une poubelle*

duster *un chiffon à poussière*

duvet *une couette*

e

ear *l'oreille*

easel *un chevalet*

eating *manger*

egg *un œuf*

eight *huit*

eighteen *dix-huit*

elbow *le coude*

elephant *un éléphant*

eleven *onze*

elf *un elfe*

empty *vide*

emu *un émeu*

engine *une locomotive*

envelope *une enveloppe*

eraser *une gomme*

evergreen plant *une plante verte*

exercise book *un cahier*

eye patch *un bandeau*

eye *l'œil*

eyebrow *le sourcil*

f

fairy *une fée*

farmer *un fermier*

farmhouse *une ferme*

fast *rapide*

fat *gros*
father *un père*
feather *une plume*
feeder cup *une timbale*
feeding bottle *un biberon*
felt pens *des feutres*
fence *une clôture*
field *un champ*
fifteen *quinze*
fig *une figue*
finger *un doigt*
fireplace *une cheminée*
first *premier*
fish *un poisson*
fish food *de la nourriture pour poisson*
fish tank *un aquarium*
fisherman *un pêcheur*
fishing boat *un chalutier*
fishing net *une épuisette*
fishing rod *une canne à pêche*
five *cinq*
fizzy drink *une boisson gazeuse*
flag *un drapeau*
flamingo *un flamand rose*
flannel *une serviette*
flask *une bouteille thermos*
flea *une puce*
flippers *des palmes*
flood *l'innondation*
flour *de la farine*
flower bed *un parterre de fleurs*
flowerpot *un pot*
flowers *des fleurs*
flute *une flûte*
fly *une mouche*
foal *un poulain*
fog *le brouillard*
food mixer *un robot ménager*
foot *le pied*
forest *une forêt*

fork (garden) *une fourche*
fork (table) *une fourchette*
fort *un château-fort*
fountain *une fontaine*
four *quatre*
fourteen *quatorze*
fridge *un réfrigérateur*
frightened (to be) *avoir peur*
frog *une grenouille*
frost *le givre*
fruit *des fruits*
frying pan *une poêle*
full *plein*

g

gale *une bourrasque*
galleon *un galion*
gate *une barrière*
giant *un géant*
giraffe *un girafe*
glass *un verre*
glove *un gant*
glove puppet *une marionnette*
goggles *des lunettes*
go-kart *un kart*
goldfish *un poisson rouge*
golf *le golf*
goose *une oie*
gooseberry *une groseille*
gorilla *un gorille*
grandfather *un grand-père*
grandmother *une grand-mère*
grapefruit *un pamplemousse*
grapes *des grains de raisin*
grasshopper *une sauterelle*
great aunt *une grand-tante*
great grandfather *un arrière grand-père*

great grandmother *une arrière grand-mère*
great uncle *un grand-oncle*
green *vert*
grey *gris*
guinea pig *un cochon d'Inde*
guitar *une guitare*
gull *une mouette*
gymnastics *la gymnastique*

h

hair *les cheveux*
hairbrush *une brosse peigne*
hamburger *un hamburger*
hammer *un marteau*
hamper *une malle*
hamster *un hamster*
hand fork *une fourche*
hand *la main*
handbag *un sac à main*
handkerchief *un mouchoir*
hangar *un hangar*
hanging basket *une jardinière suspendue*
happy (to be) *être heureux*
harp *une harpe*
hat *un chapeau*
head *une tête*
heart *un cœur*
heat *la chaleur*
heavy *lourd*
hedge *une haie*
height chart *une toise*
helicopter *un hélicoptère*
hen *une poule*
herbs *des herbes*
hi-fi *une chaîne hi-fi*
high chair *une chaise haute*

high jump *le saut en hauteur*
hill *une colline*
hippopotamus *un hippopotame*
hoe *une binette*
honey *du miel*
hook *un crochet*
hoop *un cerceau*
hooter *un klaxon*
horse *un cheval*
hose *un tuyau d'arrosage*
hot-air ballloon *un ballon dirigeable*
hotdog *un hotdog*
house *une maison*
hummingbird *un colibri*
hundred *cent*
hutch *un clapier*

i

ice *la glace*
ice cream *un cornet de glace*
ice skates *des patins à glace*
ice skating *le patin à glace*
iced lolly *une glace à l'eau*
icicles *des stalactites*
information board *un tableau d'affichage*
inside *dedans*
iris *un iris*
iron *un fer à repasser*
island *une île*

j

jacket *une veste*
Jack-in-the-box *une boîte à surprises*
jamjars *des pots à confiture*
jeans *un jean*
jellyfish *une méduse*
jetty *une jetée*
jogger *un coureur*

judo *le judo*
juggernaut *un poids-lourd*
juice *du jus de fruits*
jumper *un pullover*
jumping *sauter*

k

kangaroo *un kangourou*
kennel *une niche*
kettle *une bouilloire*
keyboard *un synthétiseur*
keyhole *un trou de serrure*
keys *des clés*
kicking (a football) *shooter*
king *un roi*
kingfisher *un martin-pêcheur*
kite *un cerf-volant*
kitten *un chaton*
kiwi *un kiwi*
knee pads *des genouillères*
knee *le genou*
knife *un couteau*
knight *un chevalier*
koala *un koala*

l

label *une étiquette*
ladder *une échelle*
ladybird *une coccinelle*
lake *un lac*
lamb *un agneau*
lamp *un lampadaire*
lampshade *un abat-jour*
lance *une lance*
lawn *un gazon*
lawnmower *une tondeuse à gazon*
lead (dog's) *une laisse*
leaping *bondir*
leaves *des feuilles*
leek *un poireau*
leg *la jambe*

lemon *un citron*
leopard *un léopard*
lettuce *une laitue*
life buoy *une bouée de sauvetage*
life vest *un gilet de sauvetage*
lift *un ascenseur*
light bulb *une ampoule*
light (weight) *léger*
lighthouse *un phare*
lightning *la foudre*
lily *un lys*
lime *une lime*
liner *un paquebot*
lion *un lion*
lip *la lèvre*
litter bin *une poubelle*
little *petit*
lizard *un lézard*
lobster *un homard*
lobster pot *un casier à homard*
log *une souche*
lollipop *une sucette*

m

magazine *un magazine*
magician *un magicien*
mallet *un maillet*
mango *une mangue*
map *une carte géographique*
maracas *des maracas*
marbles *des billes*
martial arts *arts martiaux*
mask *un masque*
mast *un mât*
mattress *un matelas*
meadow *un champ*
measuring jug *un bol-doseur*
measuring tape *un mètre-mesureur*
medicine *un médicament*
melon *du melon*

mermaid *une sirène*
message in a bottle *un message dans une bouteille*
microwave *un four à micro-ondes*
milk *du lait*
millipede *un mille-pattes*
mirror *un miroir*
mittens *des moufles*
mixing bowl *un bol mixeur*
mobile *un mobile*
modelling clay *de la pâte à modeler*
money *de l'argent*
money box *une tirelire*
monkey *un singe*
mop *un balai à franges*
moth *un papillon de nuit*
mother *une mère*
motor boat *un bateau à moteur*
motorbike *une motocyclette*
mountain *une montagne*
mouse *une souris*
mouth *la bouche*
muffin *un gâteau*
mug *une tasse*
mushrooms *des champignons*
music stand *un pupître*

n

nail brush *une brosse à ongles*
nails *des clous*
napkin *une serviette*
nappy *une couche*
navy *bleu marine*
nest *un nid*
nesting box *un nichoir*
new *neuf*
newspaper *un journal*

nightie *une robe de chambre*
nine *neuf*
nineteen *dix-neuf*
Noah's ark *l'Arche de Noé*
nose *le nez*
notes *des notes*
nurse *une infirmière, un infirmier*
nuts *des fruits secs*

o

oboe *un hautbois*
octopus *une pieuvre*
off (lamp) *éteint*
old *usé*
omelette *une omelette*
on (lamp) *allumé*
one *un*
onion *un oignon*
open *ouvert*
orange (colour) *orange*
orange (fruit) *une orange*
ostrich *une autruche*
outside *dehors*
oval *un ovale*
oven *une cuisinière*
owl *un hibou*
oyster *une huître*

p

packed lunch *une collation*
paddles *des pagaies*
page boy *un page*
paint *de la peinture*
paintbox *une boîte de couleurs*
paintbrush *un pinceau*
palm *la paume*
palm tree *un palmier*
panda *un panda*
pansy *une pensée*
pants *une culotte*

papaya *une papaye*
paper *du papier*
paper cup *un gobelet*
parachute *un parachute*
parcel *un paquet*
parrot *un perroquet*
parsnip *un panais*
party bag *une pochette-surprise*
party dress *une robe de fête*
path *un chemin*
pavement *un trottoir*
paw *la patte*
peach *une pêche*
peacock *un paon*
pear *une poire*
pearl *une perle*
peas *des petits pois*
pebbles *des galets*
pedal car *une voiture à pédales*
pelican *un pélican*
penguin *un pingouin*
penknife *un canif*
pepper *du poivre*
personal stereo *un baladeur*
photograph *une photo*
piano *un piano*
pick-up truck *une dépanneuse*
picnic *un pique-nique*
picture *un tableau*
picture frame *un cadre*
pie *une tarte*
pig *un cochon*
pigeon *un pigeon*
piggy bank *une tirelire*
piglet *un cochonnet*
pillow *un oreiller*
pilot *un pilote*
pin board *un pense-bête*
pineapple *un ananas*
pink *rose*

pipe *une gouttière*
pirate *un pirate*
pirate flag *un drapeau de pirate*
pistol *un pistolet*
pizza *une pizza*
plank *une planche*
plaster *un pansement*
plaster cast *un plâtre*
plate *une assiette*
pliers *une pince*
plum *une prune*
pocket *une poche*
polar bear *un ours blanc*
pole vaulting *le saut à la perche*
pond *une mare*
poppy *un coquelicot*
porcupine *un porc-épic*
portholes *des hublots*
portrait *un portrait*
poster *un poster*
potato *une pomme de terre*
potty *un pot*
pram *une poussette*
praying mantis *une mante religieuse*
present *un cadeau*
prince *un prince*
princess *une princesse*
proud (to be) *être fier*
puddles *des flaques*
puffin *un macareux*
pulling *tirer*
pumpkin *une citrouille*
pupil *un élève*
puppy *un chiot*
purple *violet*
purse *un porte-monnaie*
pushing *pousser*
puzzle *un puzzle*
pyjamas *un pyjama*

q

queen *une reine*

queue *une queue*

r

rabbit *un lapin*
raccoon *un raton-laveur*
racing car *une voiture de course*
radio *une radio*
radishes *des radis*
railings *une grille*
railway track *un rail de chemin de fer*
rain *la pluie*
rainbow *l'arc-en-ciel*
rake *un râteau*
raspberry *une framboise*
rattle *un hochet*
reading *lire*
recorder *un pipeau*
rectangle *un rectangle*
red *rouge*
red pepper *un poivron rouge*
refuse truck *un camion à ordures*
remote control *une télécommande*
removal van *un camion de déménagement*
rhinoceros *un rhinocéros*
rhubarb *de la rhubarbe*
ribbon *un ruban*
rice *du riz*
riding (a tricycle) *faire du tricycle*
river *une rivière*
road *une route*
robot *un robot*
rocket *une fusée*
rocking chair *un fauteuil à bascule*
rocking horse *un cheval à bascule*
rocks *des rochers*
roller skating *le patin à roulettes*

rollerskates *des patins à roulettes*
rolling pin *un rouleau à pâtisserie*
roof *un toît*
roof tile *une tuile*
rope *une corde*
rose *une rose*
rowing *l'aviron*
rowing boat *une barque*
rubber ring *une bouée*
rucksack *un sac à dos*
rug *un tapis*
rugby *le rugby*
ruler *une règle*
runner beans *des haricots verts*
running *courir*
runway *une piste d'atterissage*

s

sack race *la course en sac*
sad (to be) *être triste*
safety helmet *un casque*
salad *de la salade*
salt *du sel*
sand *du sable*
sandcastle *un château de sable*
sandpaper *du papier de verre*
sandpit *un bac à sable*
sandwiches *des sandwiches*
saucepan *une casserole*
saucer *une soucoupe*
sauces *des sauces*
sausage *de la charcuterie*
saw *une scie*

saxophone *un saxophone*

scarecrow *un épouvantail*
scarf *une écharpe*
school *une école*
schoolbag *un cartable*
scissors *des ciseaux*
scooter *une trottinette*
screwdriver *un tournevis*
screws *des vis*
sea *la mer*
sea shell *un coquillage*
seahorse *un hippocampe*
seaweed *une algue*
second *second*
security light *un projecteur*
seeds *des graines*
seesaw *une bascule*
seven *sept*
seventeen *dix-sept*
sewing machine *une machine à coudre*
shampoo *du shampooing*
shark *un requin*
shawl *un châle*
shears *des cisailles*
shed *une cabane*
sheep *un mouton*
sheet *un drap*
sheet music *une partition*
shelf *une étagère*
shield *un bouclier*
shirt *une chemise*
shoe shop *un magasin de chaussures*
shoes *des chaussures*
shop assistant *un vendeur*
shopper *un client*
shopping bag *un sac à provisions*
shopping trolley *un caddie*
short *petit*
shorts *un short*
shoulder *l'épaule*

shower *une douche*
shower curtain *un rideau de douche*
shut *fermé*
shy (to be) *être timide*
sign *un panneau*
singing *chanter*
sink *un évier*
sister *une sœur*
sitting *être assis*
six *six*
sixteen *seize*
skates *des patins*
skateboard *une planche à roulettes*
skipping *sauter à la corde*
skipping rope *une corde à sauter*
skirt *une jupe*
skis *des skis*
skittles *des quilles*
skylight *une lucarne*
sledge *une luge*
sleeping *dormir*
sleeping bag *un sac de couchage*
sleepsuit *une grenouillère*
slice of cake *une part de gâteau*
slide *un toboggan*
sling *une écharpe*
slippers *des pantoufles*
slow *lent*
slug *une limace*
snail *un escargot*
snake *un serpent*
snow *la neige*
snowflake *un flocon*
snowman *un bonhomme de neige*
soap *un savon*
soccer *le football*
socks *des chaussettes*
sofa *un canapé*
soil *de la terre*
soldiers *des soldats*
soother *une tétine*

sorry (to be) *être désolé*
soup *de la soupe*
spade *une pelle*
spaghetti *des spaghettis*
spanner *une clé*
spider *une araignée*
spider's web *une toile d'araignée*
sponge *une éponge*
spoon *une cuillère*
spots *des pois*
spring *le printemps*
square *un carré*
squirrel *un écureil*
stacking cups *des cônes*
standard lamp *un lampadaire*
standing *être debout*
star *une étoile*
starfish *une étoile de mer*
steamroller *un rouleau-compresseur*
stethoscope *un stéthoscope*
stewardess *une hôtesse*
stool *un tabouret*
storage jar *un bocal*
stork *une cigogne*
strawberry *une fraise*
streamers *des cotillons*
street light *un lampadaire*
street sign *un panneau*
stripes *des rayons*
submarine *un sous-marin*
sugar *du sucre*
suitcase *une valise*
summer *l'été*
sun *le soleil*
sun hat *un chapeau de paille*
sun cream *de la lotion solaire*
sunflower *un tournesol*

sunglasses *des lunettes*
sunshade *un parasol*
swallow *une hirondelle*
swan *un cygne*
sweet potato *une patate douce*
sweet shop *une confiserie*
sweetcorn *un épi de maïs*
sweets *des bonbons*
swimmer *un nageur*
swimming *la natation*
swimming trunks *un caleçon de bain*
swimsuit *un maillot de bain*
swing *une balançoire*
sword *une épée*
syringe *une seringue*

t

table *une table*
tablecloth *une nappe*
tablemat *un set de table*
tall *grand*
tambourine *un tambourin*
tandem *un tandem*
tangerine *une clémentine*
tanker *un camion-citerne*
tap *un robinet*
tarantula *une tarantule*
tea set *une dinette*
tea towel *un torchon*
teacher (female) *une maîtresse*
team *une équipe*
teaspoon *une petite cuillère*
teething ring *un anneau de dentition*

telephone *un téléphone*

television *une télévision*

temperature chart *une courbe de température*

ten *dix*

tennis *le tennis*

tent *une tente*

thermometer *un thermomètre*

thermos flask *une bouteille thermos*

thin *mince*

third *troisième*

thirteen *treize*

thoughtful (to be) *être pensif*

three *trois*

three-legged race *la course à deux*

thumb *le pouce*

tickets *des billets*

tie *une cravate*

tiger *un tigre*

tights *des collants*

till *une caisse-enregistreuse*

till receipt *un ticket de caisse*

timpani *des timbales*

tissues *des lingettes*

toadstool *un champignon*

toaster *un grille-pain*

toe *l'orteil*

toilet *des toilettes*

toilet paper *du papier toilette*

tomato *un tomate*

tool box *une boîte à outils*

toothbrush *une brosse à dents*

toothpaste (tube of) *un tube de dentifrice*

top (toy) *une toupie*

top (position) *au sommet*

top hat *un chapeau-claque*

torch *une lampe-torche*

tornado *une tornade*

tortoise *une tortue*

toucan *un toucan*

tractor *un tracteur*

trainer cup *une timbale*

trainers *des chaussures de sport*

trampolining *(faire du) trampoline*

trapdoor *une trappe*

tray *un plateau*

treasure *un trésor*

tree *un arbre*

trellis *une treille*

triangle (instrument) *un triangle*

triangle (shape) *un triangle*

tricycle *un tricycle*

trolley *un chariot*

trombone *un trombone*

trophy *une coupe*

trousers *un pantalon*

trowel *une truelle*

truck *un camion*

trumpet *une trompette*

trunk *un tronc*

T-shirt *un tee-shirt*

tummy *le ventre*

turkey *une dinde*

turnip *un navet*

turtle *une tortue marine*

twelve *douze*

twenty *vingt*

twins *des jumeaux*

two *deux*

u

uncle *un oncle*

up *en haut*

v

vacuum cleaner *un aspirateur*

vase *un vase*

vegetables *des légumes*

vest *un débardeur*

video *un magnétoscope*

village *un village*

vintage car *une voiture de collection*

violin *un violon*

visitor *un visiteur*

vulture *un vautour*

W

waistcoat *un gilet*

walker *un randonneur*

walking *marcher*

walking frame *un déambulateur*

walking stick *une cane*

wall tiles *des carreaux*

wallpaper *du papier peint*

wand *une baguette magique*

wardrobe *une penderie*

washbasin *un lavabo*

washing *se laver*

washing-up liquid *du liquide vaisselle*

wasp *un guêpe*

wastepaper bin *une corbeille*

watch *une montre*

water *de l'eau*

water jug *une carafe d'eau*

waterfall *une cascade*

watering can *un arrosoir*

water-skiing *du ski nautique*

waves *des vagues*

waving *saluer*

weightlifting *(soulever des) haltères*

wetsuit *une combinaison*

whale *une baleine*

wheelbarrow *une brouette*

wheelchair *un fauteuil roulant*

wheels *des roues*

white *blanc*

wind *le vent*

window *une fenêtre*

window box *une jardinière*

windsock *une manche à air*

wing *une aile*

winter *l'hiver*

wire basket *un panier*

wishing well *un puits magique*

wolf *un loup*

wooden spoon *une cuillère en bois*

woolly hat *un bonnet*

workbench *un établi*

worktop *un plan de travail*

worm *un ver*

wrapping paper *du papier cadeau*

wrist *le poignet*

writing *écrire*

X

xylophone *un xylophone*

y

yacht *un voilier*

yellow *jaune*

yogurt *un yaourt*

yo-yo *un yoyo*

Z

zebra *un zèbre*

zigzags *des zigzags*